HYMNS

WE LOVE

Hymns We Love Songbook

Copyright © Steve and Pippa Cramer, 2023

Published by:
The Good Book Company

thegoodbook.com | thegoodbook.co.uk
thegoodbook.com.au | thegoodbook.co.nz | thegoodbook.co.in

ISBN: 9781784988746 | Printed in India

Design by André Parker

CONTENTS

1. HOW GREAT THOU ART

O Lord, my God, when I in awesome wonder
Consider all the works Thy hands hath made,
I see the stars, I hear the mighty thunder,
Thy power throughout the universe displayed:

Then sings my soul, my Saviour God, to Thee,
How great Thou art, how great Thou art!
Then sings my soul, my Saviour God, to Thee,
How great Thou art, how great Thou art!

When through the woods and forest glades I wander
And hear the birds sing sweetly in the trees;
When I look down from lofty mountain grandeur,
And hear the brook, and feel the gentle breeze:

Then sings my soul...

And when I think that God, His Son not sparing,
Sent Him to die, I scarce can take it in:
That on the cross, my burden gladly bearing,
He bled and died to take away my sin.

Then sings my soul...

When Christ shall come, with shout of acclamation,
And take me home, what joy shall fill my heart!
Then I shall bow in humble adoration
And there proclaim, my God, how great Thou art!

Then sings my soul...

Carl Boberg, translated from the Swedish by Stuart K. Hine.
© 1949 and 1953 by the Stuart Hine Trust CIO.

About this hymn

- It was written in 1885 by Carl Boberg—a Swedish sailor-turned-hymn writer—under the title "O Store Gud".

- Boberg published more than 60 poems, hymns and songs, but this one is easily his most famous.

- It was translated into the English version we know and love today by Stuart K. Hine in 1948.

Exploring the Christian faith

The Bible says that the wonderful world around us points us to God, the Creator:

- He is a God who is powerful and holy, set apart from us, and…

- He is a God who loves his creation, loves us and wants a relationship with us.

"For my thoughts are not your thoughts, neither are your ways my ways," declares the LORD. "As the heavens are higher than the earth, so are my ways higher than your ways and my thoughts than your thoughts."

ISAIAH 55:8-9

Questions to consider

- How do you feel when you look at the natural world around you?

- Are there particular aspects of creation that you enjoy or marvel at?

- Why did God create all of this, and create us, do you think?

- Has the hymn made you think differently about God's holiness or his love?

Prayer

Dear Lord,

Thank you that you are a powerful, great God, who created the entire universe and trillions of stars with just the power of your word.

Thank you also that you love the beauty and detail of life, taking joy in peaceful forest glades and exquisite bird song as well as in the splendour of the lofty mountains.

Most of all, thank you that you love and take joy in your relationship with us, your people.

Help me to know your love, to experience your joy and to see the world around me, and people around me, as you do.

As I reflect on these wonderful hymns, please help me to take a step closer to you each day—to see you more clearly, love you more dearly and follow you more nearly.

In Jesus' name,

Amen

2. ROCK OF AGES

Rock of Ages, cleft for me,
Let me hide myself in Thee;
Let the water and the blood,
From Thy wounded side which flowed,
Be of sin the double cure;
Cleanse me from its guilt and power.

Not the labour of my hands
Can fulfil Thy law's demands;
Could my zeal no respite know,
Could my tears for ever flow,
All for sin could not atone;
Thou must save, and Thou alone.

Nothing in my hand I bring,
Simply to Thy cross I cling;
Naked, come to Thee for dress;
Helpless, look to Thee for grace;
Foul, I to the Fountain fly;
Wash me, Saviour, or I die.

While I draw this fleeting breath,
When mine eyelids close in death,
When I soar to worlds unknown,
See Thee on Thy judgment throne,
Rock of Ages, cleft for me,
Let me hide myself in Thee.

Augustus M. Toplady

About this hymn

- It was written by Augustus Toplady while he was serving as a curate in Blagdon, Somerset, England, in 1776.

- A popular story is that he wrote the hymn on the back of a playing card while sheltering from a storm in a cave.

- However, it is more likely that he was inspired by this verse from the Bible: "Trust in the LORD for ever, for the LORD … is the Rock eternal" (Isaiah 26:4).

Exploring the Christian faith

- Jesus was a real, historical person; he lived and died 2,000 years ago in what is now modern-day Israel.

- He claimed to be the Son of God. He said he was the way to God, the truth about God, and life itself.

- The Bible tells us that Jesus chose to die on the cross to pay the price necessary to restore our relationship with God, and to show just how loved and precious each of us is to God.

Jesus answered, "I am the way and the truth and the life. No one comes to the Father except through me."

JOHN 14:6

Questions to consider

- Did you know this hymn already? If so, what did you think about it?

- Who was Jesus? What do/can we know about him?

- Why is the cross so important to Christians?

- Has today made you think about the cross in a different way?

Prayer

Dear God,

Thank you that you chose to pour out your love on me—that through the life, death, and resurrection of Jesus, you offer to pick me up, wash me clean and make me whole.

Thank you, Lord, that all of this was done by Jesus, and none of it depends on how good, or how bad, I have been. You love me regardless, and I am priceless in your eyes.

Help me now to know and accept your kind and wonderful gift of forgiveness.

In the name of Jesus, I pray.

Amen

3. AMAZING GRACE

Amazing grace! How sweet the sound,
That saved a wretch like me!
I once was lost but now am found,
Was blind but now I see.

'Twas grace that taught my heart to fear,
And grace my fears relieved;
How precious did that grace appear
The hour I first believed!

Through many dangers, toils and snares
I have already come;
'Tis grace has brought me safe thus far,
And grace will lead me home.

The Lord hath promised good to me;
His word my hope secures;
He will my shield and portion be
As long as life endures.

When we've been there ten thousand years,
Bright shining as the sun,
We've no less days to sing God's praise
Than when we first begun.

John Newton

About this hymn

- "Amazing Grace" was written by John Newton in 1772 for a prayer service at his church in Olney, Buckinghamshire, England.

- As a younger man, he had worked on slave ships transporting enslaved people from Africa to the Caribbean.

- A near-death experience caused him to throw himself on God's grace—and this proved to be a real turning point.

- Later in life, he joined with others in campaigning for the Abolition of the Slave Trade Act (1807).

Exploring the Christian faith

- God's grace is extravagant, undeserved and… utterly wonderful.

- It goes much further and deeper than "just" forgiveness.

- It restores us to a full and close relationship with God.

"While [the son] was still a long way off, his father saw him and was filled with compassion for him; he ran to his son, threw his arms round him and kissed him … 'Let's have a feast and celebrate. For this son of mine was dead and is alive again; he was lost and is found.'"

LUKE 15:20, 23-24

Questions to consider

- What does the word "grace" mean to you?

- Can you identify with the son in Jesus' parable at all? In what way?

- What do you think about the way in which the father reacted? Is that what you expected? Do you think God could ever react to you in the same way?

- What do you think of the idea that we can have a relationship with God as our Father? What might it look like?

Prayer

Dear Lord,

Thank you that no matter how far I wander away from you, you will always be there waiting, like the father in the story of the prodigal son, ready to run towards me with your arms open wide, to pick me up, hug me and welcome me back to be at your side.

Thank you that the life of John Newton shows how this is true even for those of us who feel so undeserving.

Lord, maybe for the first or for the hundredth time, I turn to you now and say I am sorry for all that I have done wrong. Please forgive me, wash me clean and take me back into your arms.

I ask this in the name of Jesus and in confidence that you hear me and love me.

Amen

4. THE LORD'S MY SHEPHERD

The Lord's my Shepherd, I'll not want;
He makes me down to lie
In pastures green; He leadeth me
The quiet waters by.

My soul He doth restore again,
And me to walk doth make
Within the paths of righteousness,
E'en for His own name's sake.

Yea, though I walk in death's dark vale,
Yet will I fear no ill;
For Thou art with me, and Thy rod
And staff me comfort still.

My table Thou hast furnishèd
In presence of my foes;
My head Thou dost with oil anoint,
And my cup overflows.

Goodness and mercy all my life
Shall surely follow me,
And in God's house for evermore
My dwelling-place shall be.

Words: Francis Rous (after King David)
Music (Crimond): Jessie Seymour Irvine

About this hymn

- "The Lord's My Shepherd" is based on Psalm 23—a poem from the Bible written by Israel's King David.

- David started life as a shepherd boy. The psalm follows a year in the life of a shepherd and his sheep, drawing a comparison with how God cares for his people.

- The words for this version of the hymn were developed by a group of Scottish Protestants and first appeared in 1650. The tune "Crimond" was written by Jessie Seymour Irvine in 1872.

Exploring the Christian faith

Psalm 23 paints a picture of God as a loving, good Shepherd, who…

- cares for his sheep daily,

- travels every step of their lives with them, and

- will bring them safely to their eternal home.

"[God] tends his flock like a shepherd: he gathers the lambs in his arms and carries them close to his heart."

ISAIAH 40:11

Questions to consider

- Was there anything that particularly struck you from the psalm?

- Where do you feel you are at the moment: in green pastures, or the valley of the shadow, or somewhere else?

- What difference would it make if you knew that God was your Shepherd, leading you through?

- How do you feel about your life's journey going forward?

- Do you think you are able to trust God to the end of your journey?

Prayer

In the book of Romans, Paul says this: "I am convinced that neither death nor life, neither angels nor demons, neither the present nor the future, nor any powers, neither height nor depth, nor anything else in all creation, will be able to separate us from the love of God that is in Christ Jesus our Lord."

(Romans 8:38-39)

Heavenly Father,

Thank you that if I choose to follow, you will be my good Shepherd, and you will be by my side through the best times, but also through the darkest of valleys, when life feels too hard, and you promise you will never leave me.

Please draw me closer to you. Lead me, protect me, and care for me, comfort and sustain me. I trust you to lead me through the rest of my life and to be by my side, whatever happens, for now and for evermore.

In Jesus' name,

Amen

5. AND CAN IT BE?

And can it be that I should gain
An int'rest in the Saviour's blood?
Died He for me, who caused His pain?
For me, who Him to death pursued?
  Amazing love! How can it be
  That Thou, my God, shouldst die for me?

He left His Father's throne above,
So free, so infinite His grace;
Emptied Himself of all but love,
And bled for Adam's helpless race:
  'Tis mercy all, immense and free,
  For, O my God, it found out me.

Long my imprisoned spirit lay
Fast bound in sin and nature's night;
Thine eye diffused a quick'ning ray,
I woke, the dungeon flamed with light;
  My chains fell off, my heart was free,
  I rose, went forth and followed Thee.

No condemnation now I dread;
Jesus, and all in Him, is mine!
Alive in Him, my living Head,
And clothed in righteousness divine,
  Bold I approach th' eternal throne,
  And claim the crown, through Christ my own.

Charles Wesley

About this hymn

- Charles Wesley was born in 1707 as the 18th of 19 children. He wrote over 6,500 hymns in his lifetime.

- As young men, Charles and his brother John were known for taking their religion very seriously. They and their friends were nicknamed the "holy club" or "Methodists".

- Everything changed for them in 1738 when they truly encountered God's grace for the first time. "And Can It Be?" was inspired by this experience.

Exploring the Christian faith

If we're trusting in Jesus, we can be confident to draw near to God as our Father because...

- Our relationship with God does not depend on us and what we do.

- Instead, it depends on Jesus and what he has already done for us through his death and resurrection.

"Since we have a great high priest who has ascended into heaven, Jesus the Son of God ... Let us then approach God's throne of grace with confidence, so that we may receive mercy and find grace to help us in our time of need."

HEBREWS 4:14, 16

Questions to consider

- Was there anything that particularly struck you from this session?

- Have you ever known someone (perhaps it's you) who has tried to earn God's acceptance through what they do? What are the problems with that approach?

- What's different about the Christian message ("the way of done", as the talk put it)?

- If a person believes that Jesus has done everything they need for them, what kind of life will they lead?

- How do you think it would feel to put your trust completely in what Jesus has done? Is that something you've done or would like to do—or are you still thinking about it?

Prayer

My Lord and my God,

Thank you that you made me, and you love me.

Thank you that your love and acceptance isn't based on my goodness but on the goodness of Jesus and his death on the cross.

I am so sorry for the times I have lived away from your ways, and I ask for your forgiveness.

I now turn to you and accept your amazing gift of forgiveness and eternal life.

I give my life to you and ask you to be my Lord.

Please fill me with your love today and help me to live for you by the power of your Holy Spirit.

Thank you.

Amen

SEASONAL
SPECIALS

HARK! THE HERALD ANGELS SING

Hark! The herald angels sing,
"Glory to the newborn King!
Peace on earth and mercy mild
God and sinners reconciled!"
Joyful, all ye nations rise;
Join the triumph of the skies;
With the angelic host proclaim:
"Christ is born in Bethlehem!"

Hark! The herald angels sing,
"Glory to the newborn King!"

Christ, by highest heav'n adored,
Christ, the everlasting Lord!
Late in time behold Him come,
Offspring of the Virgin's womb.
Veiled in flesh the Godhead see;
Hail the incarnate Deity,
Pleased as man with man to dwell.
Jesus, our Emmanuel.

Hark! The herald angels sing,
"Glory to the newborn King!"

Hail the heav'n-born Prince
                    of Peace!
Hail the Sun of Righteousness!
Light and life to all He brings,
Ris'n with healing in His wings.
Mild He lays His glory by,
Born that man no more may die,
Born to raise the sons of earth,
Born to give them second birth.

Hark! The herald angels sing,
"Glory to the newborn King!"

Charles Wesley

About this hymn

- It was written by Charles Wesley—author of over 6,500 hymns, including "And Can It Be?"

- This carol began life in 1739. Charles' original tune was much more sombre, and its first line was "Hark how all the welkin rings, 'glory to the King of kings'".

- The words went through many revisions after Charles' death. In 1856, William Cummings adapted the words to fit a new cantata Felix Mendelssohn had written to commemorate the 400th anniversary of the printing press.

Exploring the Christian faith

The story of Christmas is the story of God's Son, Jesus, coming into our world on a rescue mission. This Christmas he offers us…

- The gift of comfort—knowing that Jesus is with us in the midst of our sadness and struggle.

- The gift of hope—as we trust in Jesus' life, death and resurrection for forgiveness, and look forward to a wonderful future with God.

"For God so loved the world that he gave his one and only Son, that whoever believes in him shall not perish but have eternal life. For God did not send his Son into the world to condemn the world, but to save the world through him."

JOHN 3:16-17

Questions to consider

- Did anything from the talk strike you in particular?

- How are you feeling about the Christmas season and the end of another year? In what ways do you need comfort and hope?

- What does it tell us about God that he would come into our world—not as a VIP but as a poor and helpless baby?

- What would it look like for you to begin to unwrap Jesus' two gifts of comfort and hope? Or are there questions that you need to have answered first?

Prayer

Dear Lord,

Thank you so much for Christmas—that 2,000 years ago you sent your son, Jesus, to be born in a stable so he could rescue the world… and also rescue me.

I ask that you help me to know your comfort and your hope this Christmas. Thank you that these gifts are ready and waiting for me—I don't need to do anything extra or special to earn them; I just need to accept them.

Please watch over me, my family and friends today and over the coming weeks, and help each of us to know your comforting presence by our side and your bright hope for a future spent with you.

In Jesus' name, we pray.

Amen

THINE BE THE GLORY

Thine be the glory, risen, conqu'ring Son;
Endless is the victory Thou o'er death hast won;
Angels in bright raiment rolled the stone away,
Kept the folded grave-clothes where Thy body lay.

Thine be the glory, risen, conquering Son;
Endless is the victory Thou o'er death hast won.

Lo! Jesus meets us, risen from the tomb;
Lovingly He greets us, scatters fear and gloom;
Let the church with gladness, hymns of triumph sing,
For her Lord now liveth: death hath lost its sting.

Thine be the glory, risen, conquering Son;
Endless is the victory Thou o'er death hast won.

No more we doubt Thee, glorious Prince of life;
Life is naught without Thee: aid us in our strife;
Make us more than conquerors, through Thy deathless love;
Bring us safe through Jordan to Thy home above.

Thine be the glory, risen, conquering Son;
Endless is the victory Thou o'er death hast won.

Edmond Budry

About this hymn

- "Thine Be the Glory" was written by the Swiss hymn-writer Edmond Budry in 1884.

- Edmond was born in Vevey—the home of milk chocolate—and later became a pastor there.

- He set the hymn to a tune composed by George Handel some 140 years previously.

- It was translated from French into English in 1923.

Exploring the Christian faith

- The claim that Jesus rose from the dead is central to the Christian message. It shows that God can be trusted, forgiveness is possible, death is defeated and heaven is attainable.

- The risen Jesus patiently and lovingly met his followers in their fear and doubt, and brought them to a place of joy and confidence—and he offers to do the same for us.

"When the disciples were together, with the doors locked for fear of the Jewish leaders, Jesus came and stood among them and said, 'Peace be with you!' After he said this, he showed them his hands and side. The disciples were overjoyed when they saw the Lord."

JOHN 20:19-20

Questions to consider

- Was there anything in the talk that particularly struck you?

- Which characters in the Easter story did you most identify with, and why?

- Why did Jesus' resurrection so transform his first followers? Why is it still significant for Christians today?

- How would you describe what Jesus is like, based on what you've heard today?

- As you consider Christianity, what questions, doubts or fears do you have? Would you be willing to bring them to Jesus and let him meet you in them?

Prayer

Dear Lord,

Thank you that no matter where I am today, you are able to find me, to come by my side and to call me by my name. Thank you that you are not put off by my doubts, uncertainty, or fears, but that because of Jesus, you will always be ready to welcome me, just as I am.

Help me now to put my trust in you, knowing that being held in your arms is the safest place to be.

I ask, dear Lord, that over the coming days, you would help me draw close to you, listen to your voice and come to know just how much you love me.

In the name of Jesus, I pray.

Amen

MY SONG IS LOVE UNKNOWN

My song is love unknown,
My Saviour's love to me,
Love to the loveless shown
That they might lovely be.
O, who am I,
That for my sake
My Lord should take
Frail flesh and die?

He came from his blest throne
Salvation to bestow;
But such disdain! So few
The longed-for Christ would
know!
But O, my Friend,
My Friend indeed,
Who at my need
His life did spend!

Sometimes they crowd His way
And His sweet praises sing,
Resounding all the day
Hosannas to their King.
Then "Crucify!"
Is all their breath,
And for His death
They thirst and cry.

They rise and needs will have
My dear Lord made away.
A murderer they save,
The Prince of life they slay.
Yet cheerful He
To suff'ring goes
That He His foes
From death might free.

In life, no house, no home
My Lord on earth might have;
In death, no friendly tomb,
But what a stranger gave.
What may I say?
Heav'n was His home,
But mine the tomb
Wherein He lay.

Here might I stay and sing;
No story so divine,
Never was love, dear King,
Never was grief like Thine.
This is my Friend,
In whose sweet praise
I all my days
Could gladly spend!

Samuel Crossman

35

About this hymn

- The words were written as a poem by Samuel Crossman, an English clergyman, in 1664.

- Following Samuel's death in 1683, the words were set to music and sung like a formal psalm for many years in Anglican churches.

- It wasn't until 1919 that it became the popular hymn we know and love today. The editors of England's *Public School Hymn Book* asked the composer John Ireland to come up with a new tune—which he's said to have done in just ten minutes on a scrap of paper!

Exploring the Christian faith

Christians believe that two things were going on during Jesus' final days:

- On a human level, Jesus was a real person who was brutally executed by the Roman authorities of his day.

- On a deeper level, God planned for this to happen. Jesus' death had a purpose—to show us God's love and to make us lovely in God's sight.

"God demonstrates his own love for us in this: while we were still sinners, Christ died for us."

ROMANS 5:8

Questions to consider

- Was there anything that particularly struck you from this session?

- We've heard that at the heart of the Christian faith is love. Is that what you would have said before this session? What word might you have chosen instead?

- Have you ever felt that God loves you? What makes you say that?

- How does Jesus' death on the cross show us God's love? What impact, if any, do you think Jesus' death has for you?

Prayer

Dear Lord,

Thank you so much for what Jesus did for us 2,000 years ago. Thank you for his life, for his sacrificial death and for his resurrection.

Thank you that through the awful hate and brutality of that last week, you showed just how much you love me.

Help me to receive and accept your love in my life and help me to allow you to change my life, so that I might be lovely in your eyes.

In Jesus' name, I pray.

Amen

Thanks for reading this book. We hope you enjoyed it, and found it helpful.

Most people want to find answers to the big questions of life: Who are we? Why are we here? How should we live? But for many valid reasons we are often unable to find the time or the right space to think positively and carefully about them.

Perhaps you have questions that you need an answer for. Perhaps you have met Christians who have seemed unsympathetic or incomprehensible. Or maybe you are someone who has grown up believing, but need help to make things a little clearer.

At The Good Book Company, we're passionate about producing materials that help people of all ages and stages understand the heart of the Christian message, which is found in the pages of the Bible.

Whoever you are, and wherever you are at when it comes to these big questions, we hope we can help. As a publisher we want to help you look at the good book that is the Bible because we're convinced that as we meet the person who stands at its heart—Jesus Christ—we find the clearest answers to our biggest questions.

Visit our website to discover the range of books, videos and other resources we produce, or visit our partner site www.christianityexplored.org for a clear explanation of who Jesus is and why he came.

Thanks again for reading,

Your friends at The Good Book Company

thegoodbook.com | thegoodbook.co.uk
thegoodbook.com.au | thegoodbook.co.nz | thegoodbook.co.in

WWW.CHRISTIANITYEXPLORED.ORG

Our partner site is a great place to explore the Christian faith, with powerful testimonies and answers to difficult questions.